Pictures at an Exhibition

AKRON SERIES IN POETRY

Titles published since 2008.
For a complete listing of titles published in the series,
go to www.uakron.edu/uapress/poetry.

Pictures at an Exhibition
A Petersburg Album

Philip Metres

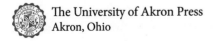
The University of Akron Press
Akron, Ohio

20   19   18   17   16   5   4   3   2   1

A catalog record for this title is available from the Library of Congress.

∞The paper used in this publication meets the minimum requirements of A N S I / N I S O z 39.48–1992 (Permanence of Paper).

Cover: *Untitled* by Eduard Gordeev, © 2015. Reproduced with permission. Cover design by Amy Freels.

Pictures at an Exhibition was designed and typeset in Minion with Avenir display by Amy Freels and printed on sixty-pound natural and bound by Bookmasters of Ashland, Ohio.

Contents

Pictures at an Exhibition: A Petersburg Album takes its name from Modest Musorgsky's moody music meant to simulate a stroll through a gallery, but the "pictures" Philip Metres describes are fraught with all the tensions that place, history, language, and self can mingle. The poems take on the harshness and vitality of contemporary Russia in its hopeful and heartless state of transition. It includes palaces and pay toilets, fairytales and current gossip, the Neva River's opulence and the coldness of the streets filled with suffering humanity of the "dear city midwifed from Peter's mind." Inventive and various in its approach to what structures a poem, there are constant risks and delights in the "album" of observations deeply informed by the emotional history of what it means to know a country, a city, and a language both translated and untranslatable. The narrator both witnesses and embodies knowledge and interrogates meaning's weighty presence. In this far-ranging chronicle of being alive to a certain place and moment, overarching shadows and traces of those famous and less so join in the music of the poems. The many voices that are invoked make these poems, even the smaller, intimate ones, waver on the brink of telling more. Eyes closed or open, our narrator "whispers" truths in the margins of the poems while the text makes claims on the reader to listen and to see purely, eyes open to the terror and the beauty, all the while using the power of his language to translate "misery as a door to pleasure."

—Maxine Chernoff, Judge of the 2014 Akron Poetry Prize

Cast in the role of the anonymous observer who, in the "Promenade" music interleaved with the pictures, walks from one painting to the next. . . . He seems to have no authority over the parade of images.
—Paul Griffiths, on Modest Musorgsky's "Pictures at an Exhibition"

Destroy this album, but save whatever you have inscribed in the margin out of boredom, out of helplessness, and, as it were, in a dream.
—Osip Mandelstam

over our heads on rickety scaffolding

First Movement. A Guided Tour

This bus will take you
Throughout this Window

To the West
This Dutch Forger's

Benighted Daydream
This Venice in Ice

So let's begin:
This is the Winter Palace

Six selves sleeping on the Neva
Their dreams the frames

Of the history of Western art:
Two thousand eyes open

Outside the Hermitage, drunk again

the painters try to keep their feet

Are you sleeping?
You missed 1762

I can't catch up with my body
Clock

Is this the
This is not the bronze horseman

The other bronze horseman
Is the bronze horseman

I hate to be the head
People look through

Look above the first floor
To the flood's watermark

on images and the unceasing light

apart to scrape the aging paint;

That scaffold worker extends
A just-lit cigarette

To another not turning
Who reaches toward the ash

1905 Bloody Sunday
They wanted an eight-hour day

A thousand people were lying dead
Get up, you've already missed

The 19th century:
Raskolnikov axing his landlady

Dostoevsky hauled
In front of a firing squad

rivering through the profligate museum's

The Tsar had staged
A last-minute reprieve & decreed

Exile to Siberia instead....
He returned to *Piter*, like a dead letter

Here was the largest cathedral
The Soviet Army bivouacked

Carving a hole in the altar
For soldiers to crap in

Splitting icons with axes
To feed the splintered faces

To warm the frostbite fingers
Does the sun ever set here?

about their feet: above all

In winter, windows glow
Casting gray slush gold

I'll spare you the Blockade
Corpses face down in the frozen street

Buttocks flesh
Scooped out

See the two punks holding beers?
That is the monument to the Second War

If I were not myself, but another,
I'd hang around there every night

The eternal flame was lit in 1957
This is the first eternal flame in Russia

of Rembrandts, the dark matter giving way

naked torso gleaming sweat

Is that a pay toilet?
The KGB building where Putin began—

We've come to the end of the tour
The Church of the Savior in Spilt Blood

No, it's not a metaphor
Where an anarchist killed the Tsar

Enjoy your stay in *Piter*
Don't forget to tour the river

The Neva never stays the same

What is the name of the river?

to ghosts of faces in burnt umber:

& gray elbows abrading

Do you have to hear everything twice?

we lay ourselves down, surrendering to gravity,

Second. Gnomus

The king ordered the three greatest artists of the realm to paint his portrait. He was badly deformed, his left eye having been gouged out and his left leg maimed. The first artist produced an impeccably accurate portrait, down to the socket of the missing eye. Outraged, the king had the artist beheaded for his insolence. The second artist, fearing the fate of the first, painted a healthy king, handsome beyond compare. The king had him beheaded for his dishonesty. Now the third artist, after a sleepless night, composed the painting that would save his life: in the picture, the king, mounted on horseback, was pictured in right profile....

layers & their unshaven faces

{   }

Something outside
burns like light

at the canal's edge
three hangovers

haunch their faces
drained & asking

for *spichki* (matches)
they are matchless—

bruise ripening
under the woman's left

eye—we watch the water
sketch the 18th century

they toss back
bottles & swallow sky

itself an image of the tenuous

{   }

Returning from Amsterdam, when the ship's supply of beer ran out, Russian sailors stumbled upon Tsar Peter the Great's *wunderkammern*, his wonder cabinet of glass-jarred curiosities: a fetus dressed in lace; a four-legged rooster; botanical landscapes built from plants and lungs; a two headed-sheep; a vial of a sleeping child, its skull removed; a handkerchief into which a skeleton "cried," made of brain tissue; a severed arm, and held in its hand, a heart; a tiny head cradled in the open jaws of a gecko—all suspended in alcohol. Who started the rumor, we don't know—that when they tipped the glasses to their mouths to slake their impossible thirst, the sailors must have closed their eyes—lips kissing the sweet wet flesh.

coats of the past: look, the unconscious

Third. Dear Lattice of Peasant Ribs

dear city midwifed from Peter's mind
dear Neva Venus your avenues of want

want nothing now your churches robed
in plastic & scaffold await transfiguration

Kazan's cathedral columns a back-
drop where purple-dyed punks mill

with provincial brides & classmates mull
swirling bustle skirts to fiddles turning

tradition to invention dear city of postcoital
light & inchoate dark dear lattice

of peasant ribs & spine your Museum
of Atheism then your Museum

of Atheism & Religion now St. Isaac's
again & swathed in green curtain

dear cocoon where have you hidden
the other me   dear sweet mouth

I cannot touch your face without
that fever again

of one winter—your winter, my winter, each

Interlude: Letter (Never Sent) to Volodya and Natasha

Lying on your bed, the only bed you'd lend me, the fevered stranger a winter train coughed out, I faced the wall-sized photograph of a waterfall so large I woke sputtering in sheets and sprays, cotton mists glittering. Mirror of the eros you made. Sudden uncle and aunt, way station for the wayward.

In the rain, in the mind, in the wind outside, where Vuillard's *Children* ignore an open door, where blues of greens come to nothing we can settle into names. Natasha, do you still watch "East of Eden," read the journals of Sofia Tolstoy, make frayed ends meet?

On the train, in the bed, on the mend. Art, you said, was a sacred place, resting by a river, where a person could feel. Some things come clearer. Not better, but clearer. Volodya, remember the noir we watched? I understood enough to know I'd missed the obvious clue.

I'm still looking for it, twenty years later, listening to the singing monk you played for me on a gramophone—his voice so consumed in suffering, it lifts above his untouched body. The old needle still holds fast inside the circling groove.

It's true, Volodya, the soul is not yet complete. Is it ever?

Your eyes, stones in the bed of irreversible river.

but the upper reaches:

Scratched Track List for Hieromonk Roman's "Holy Psalter"

My soul, why are you [   ]
Night [   ]
[   ] shall vanish [   ] the eyes

    He feels he must be a ringer of bells

O [   ] Mother [God-Maker]
Rome exults in [drinking games] [revels]
Let them rejoice at my [   ] [troubles]

    For singing is leaving / the cell for the bell-tower

[   ] I am [one] [alone] again
Night [   ]
And the [   ] [zvon] of bells

    To give the people a thread to follow

Why are you [sleeping] [dreaming]
In [   ] the darkest hour
[   ] stand before the [   ]

[   ] bare
[   ] holy psalter

you came, and here we could sit and break

one hugs the prow of the building

Russian Haiku

the Roma mother
who mistook you for a son
you mistook for a Roma

open a loaf of black bread so fragrant

Fourth. Questions for Custine (The Old Haunts)

> *Customs officer: What is your object in Russia?*
> *Marquis de Custine: To see the country.*
> *Customs officer: That is not a motive for traveling here.*

What were you after?

The unwind of the watchkeeper, unhinge of the doorman.

Did you pay no attention to the man behind the curtain?

There was no curtain.

When did you stop looking?

Stop looking?

Did you mark the forty-day with pancakes and candles, when the soul severs the body's chains?

I almost hated to eat it. As if

I am still here, gone forever.

At least you have your hell. When does the mirror of train windows stop reflecting?

It is night and the blinds are drawn.

You wracked in the black of Moscow fevers?

I could not escape my circumference, packed in bags.

Is the bed of the sleeping car too narrow for sleep?

And the train of images will not stop.

Is this your version?

A monk without a cell key. A car, driving without headlights. A man without eyes.

consuming a thing meant it was lost, and not

suspended from lines they sway in

Will the chains loosen by movement?

The gilt of seeming.

And if the chains fall?

The guilt of seeing.

And when it breaks?

Another station. A couple from Chernobyl, the picture of a child they pass back and forth, as if it were alive.

And when it breaks?

When the body begins to consume itself—that's what the child had.

Sausage, bread, and sugary tea in tall glasses?

that it would become us. I hadn't loved

Yes, and thank you, and the child's cell counts, the chain of x.

What were you after?

Misery as a door to pleasure.

Vot. Another station. Someone enters, the couple leaves.

On the Street of the Stray Dog, no one could find stray dogs.

Who said, *We're all drunks and harlots here?*

It was underground so they could pretend nothing mattered but art.

Who stopped reading the story when someone in the crowd had a seizure?

I can't remember if the story was finished.

anyone yet—I hadn't fucked a soul

Who said, *Bring me a ladder. Quickly, a ladder!*

Gogol, for instance, never finished the story, or the manuscript was never found.

Is seizure a kind of possession, or abstention?

I could not find a converter, even the currents were different, and batteries did not last.

Who could not see through to the end of your travels, your three-month three-volume book of Russia, the bookmark still intact on page seventy-five, a temporary pass dated to expire 1994?

It doesn't matter how long you stay if you never leave.

Did you see the film in which a man in Moscow passes out on New Year's Eve, and his friends drag him in his stupor to the airport, and arriving in Leningrad, he hauls himself home, enters a building that must be his building, and on his proper floor, slips his key in the proper door, and it opens?

i.e., I had not yet entered the gates

Another station.

You are free to remember because you have forgotten.

Looking, looking.

What is the word in Russian for when you bite something that makes your mouth ache?

Looking, looking.

Will the Russians be satisfied?

You were with me, imperial eye.

Is it a useful journey for any foreigner?

A useless journal for every naïf and nayer.

awake & sandblast the years

What were you after?

The consummation deception assumes no mask.

What were you after?

If you are lost, just ask.

That which guards its language like a border?

That which guards its boarders like a language.

And what of the walls of grim faces?

Happiness is a spectacle.

Did you sit together for a silent moment?

Did it pass you, and glide through a gate into the courtyard?

and tangled in another's limbs. Outside

when it begins, the daily

Into the honeycomb of identical buildings, where you could not follow?

the palace walls, a boy sketched your portrait

Interlude: Letter (Never Sent) to G.

Dear G!

Why is it, in Russian letters, the direct address is always followed by an exclamation? I am not shouting at you. But there is always some question, since the postman's decade-long vodka bender, the pond full of letters.

When I met M— I— in Petersburg, he grinned as if he'd seen me buck-naked. He turned to his buddy and said: *This guy visited Gandlevsky's dacha in white shorts, with tennis racket in duffel bag.*

How the fuck does he know what I wore? Am I the long lost son of the main character (a Russian poet, very much resembling you) of your novel, who comes from America to visit his father, and not knowing the ways of the country and the dacha, arrived at the door in ridiculous short white shorts and holding a tennis racket?

I am not your son.

Having lived in your country, I knew that there wasn't a tennis court within a duck's fuck of any dacha except Yeltsin's. I did not bring a goddamned tennis racket. On the issue of the shorts, okay. They were probably beige.

Yours,

for a thousand rubles. *Later, it disappeared,*

Fifth. Promenade: Nevsky Prospekt

Elixir of walking—
gulyat': to stroll
or to get drunk—

we drink in the light
& light, & drink again—
no negative to burn

in the urn of us, sun-
stunned dream-walkers
along the Prospekt—

promenade & rendezvous
for all the idlers
etching each other inside—

three aunt-muses rouge
an ivory-wrapped
bride, the groom

skulks back, in full silks
hailing a cig—
exhaling, glazing

an image of the self you no longer

stretched across the street, a banner—

at the open
briefcase of Slims /
Reds / Lights—

the man in Armani, cell
sea-shelling
his ear, talks as if

to everyone, this tide
of bodies, eyes
a woman's gauzy blouse

blossoming
possibility—
her stilettos slashing

old gray
faces, the staid
faith in queues—

as daily penance
petticoated prostitutes still
sweep the dawn

-struck street of night's
splintered glass—
litter of glimmers—

saw yourself in—another ruin of

ПАРУСА БИЗНЕСА!

Gogol saw
everything here
as dream—a score of eyes

scouring the haze—
steam rising
from gray backs

of the wolfpack idling
exhaust at a traffic light—
yet one man

saunters the pocked
walk his umbrella
a pendulum

his rose bouquet
gripped face down—
as if he could save

the color from draining—
on one hand you've been here
on the other it wasn't you

nor was it here & thus
the man now inside
the frame has turned to

representation, the Hermitage

THE SAILS FOR BUSINESS!

look: no looking
's free: impossible
to navigate Nevsky

& take a snapshot
without *babushka*
giving you the finger

of scabbed facades, where lovers congregate

Interlude: Three Russias

1.

A New Russian approached a girl and asked her to go out with him. She asked, "Well, do you have a two-story dacha?" "No," he glumly replied. She asked, "Do you have a Mercedes Benz?" No, he didn't. Dejected, he went home and asked his old man what to do. "Oh, just knock a couple stories off your dacha, trade in your limousine, and you'll be fine."

2.

On the train, someone asks an old pensioner how things are going. "I'm getting by," he replied. "In the morning I don't eat breakfast, for lunch I drink tea with a little bread, and for dinner I take something a little less heavy."

3.

Evening was setting in, and the host offered to drive his guest home. It was a cold night, and the windshield kept icing over. Twice they almost crashed into an oncoming car, and the nervous guest advised the host to scrape off the ice. "I doubt it would help," answered the driver, "seeing as I forgot my glasses at home."

in the generous unbroken light

wood planks must be unpainted

Sixth. Gardens: A Retranslation

Behind one's back,
sight unseen—

quite enough.
Alone with one

another. To stare.
To glossy. Eye

socket. Peep

Two missionaries got home and discovered their apartment had been robbed. They called the police. When the police arrived the missionaries walked around the apartment, showing them that everything was gone except for a camera, untouched on the mantle. When the police left the missionaries sat down. Now the camera was missing—

hole. Tonsils

swollen. Voice
in the wilderness

icing over.
As the saying

goes. Openly.

in the brief season that knows no night.

Interlude: Iconostasis of the Former Museum of Atheism

Образ. Образ. Образ.
These are the faces

staring down our faces.
No cracks will show

their expression
-lessness. Each sacred image

is doom & door. Is wind
& bound to the invisible

precipice. Like a name,
it looms—not you

& yet you. How to rupture
into usable scraps, ritual

to hew
to?

How many engagements we missed, tour boats

Seventh. The Peasant Cart
(Along Griboyedov Canal)

between two stone griffins
splaying golden

wings the policeman
shrugs his shoulders

straightens his descended
arms & zips his fly—

& then struts past Tsar
Peter cigs that hang

from stoned kids' lips
dropping lines to hook

what moves inside
the dead poet's canal—

{　}

Griboyedov, in Russian, means *one of the mushroom-eaters*. His name snakes from Moyka to Fontanka, from *cleanse* to *fountain*, from Mars Field to Akhmatova's house. During the nine-hundred-day siege of Leningrad in the Great Patriotic War, everyone starved. The dogs disappeared; the cats disappeared; then even the birds. People ate anything. Someone saw a corpse in the street whose buttocks had been scooped out, like a bowl of earth where mushrooms clustered. At the canal, Moldavsky found himself entering a frozen trolley. Three people were inside, stacked like cordwood. Moldavsky and three corpses continued along the canal. What I know of Griboyedov I know from Pushkin's story, which I know from a poem by Gandlevsky. In the Caucasus mountains, at the margins of the empire, Pushkin stopped a wagon hauling a coffin to ask who it was. The driver murmured: *Griboyedov.* A Persian mob, enraged by rumors that he was harboring women who'd fled a harem, had stormed the Russian embassy.... Only because of the scar on his hand—a wound he'd received in a duel— could they put a name to the flesh they found.

even their jaws working

{   }

a *bábushka*
wearing *babúshka* hunches
behind a cart

lugging a yellow
tank of *kvass*, as if she were
feeding herself

to the machine—
how a mouse leans to open
the jaw of the snake—

she lifts her face
only after I snap
the shot

or stay on the side we knew. Like the poem

{   }

Across an empty street, a door opens like a mouth. Someone emerges, wrapped entirely in white bandages—only his eyes showing. He sprints across the street, chased by two men, and now past me, frozen and fumbling in my backpack for camera. His eyes ablaze—by madness or laughter? One grabs a trailing bandage, and they wrap him in their arms, drag him back across the street, and stuff him back inside the open door. The door slams, a mouth without words.

look down elbow ribs

Interlude: Vodka Proverbs

what have we learned
from *The Chronicle of Fires?*

before the bottle
all are equal

that vodka be rated
on the following scale:

good
& very good

first glass like a stake
the second a snake

the third is all
darling little birdies

if you are not free
you will drink

when you drink
you are free

all our plans kept ending in a door, closed

over the frantic black Benz

like a hot rose
unfolding in your chest (G.)

forbid it and it will
burn your house down

seize its throat it will
burn your house down

you don't hope
to contain it

(some call her
Ms. Swaggers in a Glass Jacket)

never leave a glass
empty on the table

never leave a bottle
not fully emptied

never leave an empty
bottle on the table

if you're coming down
with chills fill it up

if you're a little up
knock some down

for repairs. Except the two tickets

after the last vodka
watch your socks

drying in the oven
like blackened salmon

watch the steam
rise upstream don't slip

back into dream
vodka how close you are

to *water (voda)*
my dear little water

my dear little fire
-water how you ignite

my parched
voice vase

how everything burns
before it awakens

everything burns
to wake

to Pictures at an Exhibition *slipped*

Eighth. Promenade: When You Meet the Roma at the River

your face translates
       for river and ever
translates your fate

sign her your sins
       and ever forgiver
sings she your sins

pay her your pay
       for debtors endeavor
to spit in the river

your sins will be
       and severed forever
spat into the river

unlike the river
       a mirror reflecting
its framing forever

your sins will be
       just spit in the river
you'll probably live

wings swig the sky

Interlude: Questions for G.
(To Ask Upon Our Reunion)

A swallow or a gulp

Do you drink the water in St. Petersburg

Is this idiomatic

Is it rainy in Moscow now

Do you still swim in the same river

Who is this woman you hold at your side

Ms. Swaggers-in-a-glass-jacket

Slang or invention

Did they remove the brain tumor

with the years. Musorgsky's homage to a friend,

& dangle their fate beneath

Was it successful

What if it's boiled

Frozen, and boiled again

Was it *The Last* Day *of Pompeii*

The frame of the painting, larger than this apartment

Was it fire raining down

Or splitting in the earth

Opening the Head or *Trepanation of the Skull*

Remember the students on the roof, thick as hair

Is this the famous "scudding" in Russian scansion

recently dead, each movement resurrecting

the curtain the building rising

How would you translate this:

Lead, read, bed, dread—

Suggestion of narrative

Did you sleep well on the train

The heartbeat of fibrillating train tracks

When you ask a friend, how are they to answer

Do you mean nature or suture

Is Aizenstadt your father

Or the dream of a father

his now-lost watercolors, as if

like an aging bride in her veil:

Is Lena still your wife

Or the dream of a wife

When do you depart

Is this idiopathic

Remember how, just before it shattered on the cement porch

The glass bounced once

Do you have two kinds of eyes

Will I see you again

Do you hear the starlings when they don't sing

Idiom or invention

through music, he could let us see again

calafalco, *a platform, falls*

Are you not drinking now

Would you like another

Only today

Should one impart what one partially observes

How will I see you again

Was Pompeii destroyed in a single afternoon

The fires and writhing and lilac dusk

The small window in the shower is hell to open

Or opens to hell

When will you return

what no longer existed, and let it

from catar, *to watch, falls from*

Will I follow

exist again: the recurring theme

captare, *to view, a stage from which*

Interlude: Insomnia

The writer knows himself	when I thought
as he was twenty years ago	I was writing
and he has also in mind	about someone else
a vision of what he would be	I was writing
someday. Oh, one day!	about myself
But the thing he never knows	when I thought
and never dares to know	I was writing
is what he is	about myself
at the exact moment	I was writing
that he is	someone else

a movement of walking, its irregular

to see some spectacle of outside

Ninth. Ballet of the Unhatched

a man bearing
    bread transit
        on his shirt—

if I translate correctly—
    lifts the carcass
        of a stroller

from a dumpster
    puzzles over
        the circus of its joints

so many wrong ways
    to hold a thing
        in your mind

outside the pay toilet
    under the columns of Kazan
        a mother lifts her palsied boy

gait how we pass through a gallery

inside or was it inside out

from behind & under the arms
    swings him like a dancer
        into his wheelchair—

another crumb
    in the woods of memory
        the blackbird may find—

years later you will read
    this daily album
        & find absolutely

nothing you remember & everything
    so clear will be
        nowhere & nothing

like the odorless smolder
    in Peter's mind
        that flared into this city—

& near the Square of Courage
    a Pedigree ad:
        how much do we differ

strung along painting to painting:

from dogs? We sniff
      with our eyes
            to find any meat—

at Lenin Square
      the clock hands stalled—
            time the revolution began—

attach counterweights to secure places

Tenth. Club-X, Before the Bridges Lift (Two Views)

Between the gaping double-doors of *Club-X* and two leather thugs, a cardboard babe hoists head-sized steins before each suggested breast. I want to enter, be hauled into the mouth, haul it all into my mouth. Mandelstam: *The way Tatars bathe their horses, lower your eye into what will be.* Across the street, at Neva's edge, a local artist watercolors the Palace bridge, its wings splaying to twilight. *Remember the eye—a noble, but stubborn animal.* The river's colors blur with each stroke, bleed into shore. The waters rise. Everything wants to be flooded. Every empire dies, entering its own dilated eyes.

of strings, gravitas of a sustained bass

Eleventh. The Marketplace

One loaf of black bread	5 rubles
White Nights ice cream cone	6 rubles
Two Metro tokens	12 rubles
Snickers bar	14 rubles
Nine liters of water	99 rubles
Aquarium CD	100 rubles
Two street pirozhkis	9 rubles
Chicken Kiev at the Literary Café	160 rubles

{   }

Still the Old Believers / live by bread & salt alone
& refuse to use a knife / to cut the body of Christ

hauling a load take the inside plank

{   }

A recent Russian joke, "Cowboy with a Conscience": A cowboy was riding in the West when he came upon some Indians. His conscience said, "Take off your jeans." So he did. The Indians shot an arrow into his eyes. Lying on the ground, bleeding, he asked his conscience why it told him to do that. It replied, "Can't you see, your jeans are still spotless!"

{   }

Along Griboyedov Canal:
GO AWAY U.S.A.

& window sign:
1+1=1

the children's taunts in the gardens, a cart

{   }

From her excessive curiosity, an old woman tumbled out a window, fell, and shattered. Another old woman leaned out from a window and looked below at what had shattered, but from excessive curiosity also tumbled out, fell, and shattered. Then a third old woman tumbled out a window, then a fourth, then a fifth. When the sixth old woman tumbled out, I got tired of watching them and went to Maltsev market, where I heard an old blind man was given a knitted shawl.

lean inward only

{   }

Creeley & Pen
dining al fresco

across the canal, a body
adorning the lawn

a round of vodka
chased with pickled

something
it is not moved

a round of shots it is
not moved

main dish in mushrooms
it is not

moved everything
moves around it

the scherzo of an incomplete ballet

Twelfth. Catacombs of the Eye

On the ocean floor, find it. In the corner
store near the frozen dumplings, press it

into service. Soak the local: anarchy of milk
on a May Day tablecloth, the curtainless

shower swamp, the hand-twisted shirts
dripping from every curtain rod, an empty

rental flat. Outside, imbroglio of iron
flowers on canal fences above time

-sledged sidewalks. The rising canals
spill past stiletto-flexed calves

of street walkers, their moving picture
-esques. Sitting at attention, the veteran

of amputations, his glacial blue gaze,
his military cap in his lap like a sponge for change.

The glue-sniffing urchins slouched
on the crumbled window ledge

scaffolding & orchestration:

        of the Currency Exchange, their faces
        all edges. Their gray frames ashiver,

        memorized, seized birds. The water
        rises. Glut of the mouth, the eyes.

the curled fruit of another self folded

Thirteenth. *Cum Mortuis in Lingua Morta:* Awaiting G.

fabled Fountain
House—fractured brick & barrows
in weeds—a work

in digress—where
Akhmatova slept & swept after
the Revolution—

I turn past echoes
into lush garden & tongue
of paths snaking—

& inside the crowd
awaits the appointed
hour & no poet

outside *Adam & Eve*
twist in suggestive cellophane
their hands bound

to each other—
heads missing—I await
what I will say

into your self, and those two young lovers

descending ladders

in my other tongue—
how many winters
we've seen since

each other
or *did you my words*
receive—

& then you enter
where a stone mouth's
wired to a bough—

its lips will never open

somewhere swim in the blind caverns of us,

{   }

Descend the black
inexorable escalator

lit with whitened teeth
promises of new breath

to bleach away the years
& pose new eyes

slogans like candles
blazing in skulls

some of us are rising
some of us are falling

statued in this under
-ground cathedral stained

glass shattering a new
mosaic we can't piece back

everything we have taken in, dissolved

Interlude: Second Letter (Never Sent) to G.

Dear G!

When you came into the hall, I saw you as the way back, anchor for an anchorite starving on image alone. Sail to what I was, still stranded on the Island of Sight. Where I played a game with expats we called "How Many Dead People Have You Seen?" Was it a way to frame the obvious deaths—the man slumped at the steering wheel, face pressed against windshield?

You spoke your poems by heart; I read the translation. Translation: I had no voice until you began to read. I was door to what you would be, if you were somebody you never were. Your basso monotone mined line after line from your head. My translations mangled a music which means nothing but itself.

Your voice sounded like it did in the countryside, at night, when I awoke, vibrating through a bedroom wall, twining your wife's.

Forgive me what I could not say.

Yours,

to their dull minerals, quicken in us.

Fourteenth. Outside Kresti Prison

a woman conducts
    a movement for clouds
        in the key of Cyrillic

        after each flourish returns
    her finger to its original
position & pauses

to watch for the locked
    beyond stone walls
        to beckon

        the prison like a clock
    stopped & gnawing
the cuckoo inside

the empty courtyard
    orchestra pit of
        dumpster & clothesline

        her language an arrow
    arcing an invisible
word made marrow

Somewhere swims that friend, who pulled me out

a circle of painters

in the far barred
window a hand
she could find

in a photograph of hands
flagging *understand*
I understand

smoke-sphere of cigarette
delivered from lungs
she once breathed for

how long can she stand
under & sign
her life on this invisible

line

from a dark pit, inexplicable winter

Interlude: Letter to Petersburg

window to the wistful you kept me

up at nights your light tethered

me to beds unmateable untranslateable

your schoolchildren threw snowballs

over the mass grave at Piskariovsky

apparition of Gandlevsky shaking

shaking Gogol & Dostoyevsky

daymares the neural galleries & sculleries

of fevers, then disappeared himself. Somewhere

lying & cannot lift his body

I lose & lore you unowned & owed

your cold mouth your winter eyes I wanted

to erase my face in your face ascending as I

descended the escalator sans guile & lyre

turning so I could see what I would

lose forever saffron insides of apartments

you bled your gold & gilded the gray outside

where my words herd not the you of you

an old song harped on a strand of sand

where torn plastic tarps like sails

all the images have thrown out their seeds

lift his eyes can't lift

ghost ship of a building skeleton

flagellate the stone, shred themselves a history

of inward windows O windward gate

locked & jawed I've gotten no closer to you

than to my death! here, at the river of never

I want to burn posthumously like a word

to say farewell & beg forgiveness

in one breath & cede you to you

return whatever I've taken

this sudden blood on my tongue

into the four directions of the self, their roots

his body from this city

if only to lift the holy psalter of you

& kneel before the soiled altar of you

& open my broken throat

sleeping inside their shells. What has not yet

Fifteenth. Vereshchagin's *Doors*

All entrances forbid. But I linger
        before the enormous
gold arabesques of painted doors
        in *The Doors of the Mosque*—

as if by following the lines
        to their end, I might enter
what I couldn't understand.
        Ten years since I first stood

dizzied by its beggars—one
        cross-legged, hands working
over something not visible, face
        turned away. Half in terror

they might return his gaze,
        Vereshchagin must have hurried
back to sketch them still
        blazing the edges of his sight.

A world so far from where he came,
        that, upon arrival, he was
someone else. How he fled, could not
        but return in his mind again

existed, let it fist forth, probe its feet

to the country he was born to paint
    and throw himself against,
his brush retouching the hands that lifted
    as he passed them daily, brushing

his sides, as if he were a canvas.
    It's not my place, he'd want
to say. Or, *I can't understand.* The gold
    minaret ablaze, the beggar

soured in filth, his hand a child's mouth.
    Judging eye. Window
without frame. Why do I turn my face again
    to what looks away?

Years ago, in winter, so sick
    it hurt to inhale, in the shell
of what I did not know
    I was, I stumbled on a station—

its five tracks stretching
    past the horizon, took the thumb
to St. Petersburg, tilted
    with the crowd past a legless vet,

his palm open as if holding up
    the globe. I went inside,

into this dream of life, in due time.

lashes curtains

saw the doors, and they did not
      open. I stood at the doors,

and they did not open—and I could rest,
      at last, before them.

What has not yet come to open its eyes,

won't fall down

read the map of its lids, memorize

they must be lowered by a merciful hand

the symphony of its mother's body

Coda. At the Dump with Van Gogh's *Peach Tree in Blossom*

—for Olga Leontievna Lepedina

because his daubed blooms
leap still
along scrawl of limb

        as twenty years ago, at tether

                                        end—

because his peach tree hoists
& hosts a mauve blaze

& the earth beneath
roils to a froth under his palette knife

        as twenty years ago my I—

& even the cockeyed fence posts lunge
to be undone by that impasto sky

        twenty years—

        wanderjahr of shock
        capitalism & still-Stalinist cashiers
        behind closed grills at end-
        of-the-line train depots
        Snickers bars & statue graveyards

        where I tried to live a year

like a Russian
if a Russian
were bootless & coatless—

because from Russia to Amsterdam in spring & everything
suddenly too easy, machinery
of late capitalism lubed
& so smoothly

the machine is unseen & all-seeing—open-armed
bridges & sidewalk cafés & glassed-in
lingeried Natashas
drowsing on bar stools without bars—

year of midnight tea to quell delirial chills
after post-Soviet winter of diesel cough
same old new brutalism & permafrost
mushroom hunting & crumpled piles of Lenin
rubles gray ice the onion domes of
drunks & dumpsters overflowing

because ruin
is the mother of future

& Olga dear physicist babushka
oven-warm & worried
over my arctic dark & day sweats
with your blue nervous big-breasted kindness

in your our sultry two-bedroom
apartment of knitting magazines & broken-
egged breakfasts left for your insomniac
word-weary non-son you doted on
more than your own

you'd say, *you're an impressionable*
person you need
to rest

after the unspeaking overcoated crowds after
stone elbows after the solid exhaust after the lying
& the lyres all pawned or hidden

you'd say, *don't write too soon*
what takes a life
to say

after the coup of coupons when ex-Party
oligarchs bought everyone's share for kopecks
because everyone feared everything
Soviet would be worthless

& everyone could be bought
& everyone fucked
up or over—

as if the whole country were tilting
then tipping
into ice—

because at the Van Gogh Museum
I took home *Peach Tree in Blossom*
thinking of you—

the print buckles, heavy with humidity
greens & blues & clears
yellowed like midlife teeth & too much tea—

because pain haunts the mention—

because paint hints dimension
the print could never show
except when swallowing
the very air—

    & in Amsterdam the buildings flowed
    upside-down in the canal
    like currency—

        Olga, dear cold-fingered in unheated labs

        you stayed

& everywhere spring now
immolating winter

& at a Cleveland dump twenty years later
with a trunkload of broken-framed basement prints

        because Olga I failed by leaving & leaving
        you & what I had been

because botched copy of all that blazing

        I refuse to leave you

& yet I leave you again

Notes

This is a work of friction. One surface: St. Petersburg, Russia, during the summer solstice of 2002, the year before the city's 300th anniversary. "Here, everything has been created for visual perception." Madame de Staël, Mr. Ashbery, apologies for *ut pictura poesis*. Another surf: Musorgsky's *Pictures at an Exhibition*, also called *Album Series on the genius architect Hartmann*. Another surfeit: a reunion with the poet Sergey Gandlevsky (my G.), whose collected poems I'd translated, at the Anna Akhmatova Museum in Fountain House. Another earth is: a photo album. Outer façade: wordswords. Utter fiction: a daughter's eyes, *in utero*.

The titles of the sections borrow from or echo the titles to the movements of Modest Musorgsky's *Pictures at an Exhibition*, completed July 4, 1874.

First Movement. A Guided Tour
Roving through the exhibition, now leisurely, now briskly in order to come close to a picture.

Lines borrowed from a tour guide, from Michael Leong, and from Sergey Gandlevsky.

The *Bronze Horseman* is both a sculpture of Peter the Great by Falconet (1782) and the name of a famous poem by Alexander Pushkin (1833). Blok once said, "We all exist in the vibrations of its bronze" (qtd. in Volkov, *St. Petersburg: A Cultural History*, 25). However, a second horseman in bronze (Alexander III, 1909), completely different in appearance, was moved nearby in 1994. Its sculptor, Trubetskoy, was known to have said, regarding the hippopotamus-like appearance of his tsar, "I don't care about politics. I simply just depicted one animal on another" (qtd. in Volkov, *St. Petersburg: A Cultural History*, 216).

Alexander Griboyedov, a poet known for *Woe from Wit*, was ambassador to Persia when he came to an untimely end, after harboring three Armenians who had fled a harem.

Joseph Brodsky: "You cannot enter the same river twice, even if it is the Neva River" (qtd. in Volkov, *St. Petersburg: A Cultural History*, xxi).

Second. Gnomus
Three savagely differing musics—violently convulsive, forcefully leaping and stumbling, menacingly creeping.

For Dimitri Psurtsev, co-conspirator, who made the original "den of the voice."

Peter the Great's wonder cabinet collections included the specimens of Frederik Ruysch, a Dutch botanist and anatomist. The rumor that sailors drank the alcohol containing the specimens has persisted to this day, though most sources believe it to be untrue.

Third. Dear Lattice of Peasant Ribs
More muted and soft than the first.

During the Soviet period, St. Isaac's became The Museum of Atheism. During the early post-Soviet years, it became The Museum of Atheism and Religion. Now it is St. Isaac's again, and The State Museum of the History of Religion has its own building.

Scratched Track List for Hieromonk Roman's "Holy Psalter"
Hieromonk Roman is a Russian monk whose record "I Shall Open the Holy Psalter" was passed along to me.

Fourth: Questions for Custine (The Old Haunts)
Performer must guard against monotony of the piece.

Marquis de Custine, a French aristocrat who visited Russia in 1839, wrote a three-volume account of his travels and seemed prophetic during the Soviet period. Custine: "The more I see of Russia, the more I approve of the Emperor in forbidding his subjects to travel, and in rendering access to his own country difficult for foreigners."

The Irony of Fate was a Soviet film in which a man from Moscow, drunk from pre-New Year's partying, is put on a plane to Leningrad. He's so plastered he fails to see—when he takes the identical streets to the identical apartment complex and staggers up to the identical flat—that he's not in Moscow at all.

Interlude: Letter (Never Sent) to G.
Sergey Gandlevsky's *[Illeg.]*, a novel, was published in 2002.

Fifth. Promenade: Nevsky Prospekt
Simple, strong rhythms, but a changing meter.

Nevsky Prospekt is the main thoroughfare in St. Petersburg, running perpendicular to the Neva River.

Custine: "[Nevsky Prospekt] serves as a promenade and rendezvous for all the idlers of the city."

"Just like that youth ends…" is adapted from Sergey Gandlevsky.

Joseph Brodsky: "Any experience coming from the Russian realm, even when depicted with photographic precision, simply bounces off the English language, leaving no visible imprint on its surface" (*Less Than One*, 30).

Strictly speaking, she gave me the "evil eye."

Interlude: Three Russias
Three selected *anekdoty* (jokes) I read during the "Wild 90's" in Russia.

Sixth. Gardens: A Retranslation
Hartmann's picture of the Jardin des Tuileries in Paris is now lost.

Thanks to Garrick Infanger for his anecdote of the camera.

Interlude: Iconostasis of the Former Museum of Atheism
Образ means icon, image, and way (as in the expression, "way of life"). Leontius of Neapolis once said that icons are "open books to remind us of God."

Seventh. The Peasant Cart (Along Griboyedov Canal)
Melancholic and rumbling.

Dmitry Moldavsky's story is found in *The 900 Days*.

Pushkin's encounter with the corpse of Griboyedov is told in his *Journey to Arzrum*.

Kvass is a Russian drink made from fermented rye grain; once popular, it fell out of favor until recently reborn as a nostalgia drink.

Interlude: Vodka Proverbs
The Chronicle of Fires demonstrates that a drastic rise in catastrophic fires occurred in the city simultaneous to the introduction of vodka into Russian society.

Most of the proverbs are translations from the Russian, which has hundreds of proverbs about drinking.

The line "like a hot rose / unfolding in your chest" comes from a poem by Sergey Gandlevsky.

Eighth. Promenade: When You Meet the Roma at the River
Tranquillo.

Interlude: Questions for G. (To Ask Upon Our Reunion)

What to ask a poet you know but do not know, and how to say it?

Nineteenth-century Russian artist Karl Briullov's epic painting, *The Last Day of Pompeii*, was taken by some as a prophecy for St. Petersburg's eventual demise.

Interlude: Insomnia

Words borrowed from William Carlos Williams ("Spring & All") and Osip Mandelstam.

Ninth. Ballet of the Unhatched

Балет невылупившихся птенцов. The fledglings were canary chicks.

Tenth. Club-X, Before the Bridges Lift (Two Views)

Two Jews, rich and poor . . . dual portrait and dramatic incident.

The italicized lines come from *Journey to Armenia* by Osip Mandelstam. Also: "I would recommend the following method of looking at pictures. Under no circumstances go in as if you were entering a chapel. Don't be thrilled or chilled and don't get glued to the canvas. With the stride of a stroll on a boulevard: straight on!"

Eleventh. The Marketplace

Bustling.

"Creeley & Pen" refers to a story I heard from Penelope Creeley.

The final section is a translation of a prose poem by Daniil Kharms, who died during the Siege of Leningrad.

Twelfth. Catacombs of the Eye

Examining catacombs by the light of a lantern.

St. Petersburg, built on a swamp next to the Baltic Sea, has flooded a number of times throughout its history; the flood of 1824, in which the city took on thirteen feet of water in a single night, was immortalized in Pushkin's *The Bronze Horseman*.

Thirteenth. *Cum Mortuis in Lingua Morta*: Awaiting G.

With the Dead in a Dead Language.

Musorgsky: "The creative spirit of Hartmann leads me toward the skulls, calls to them—the skulls begin to shine."

The Anna Akhmatova Museum, part of the former Sheremetev Palace, also called the Fountain Palace, is located where Akhmatova lived for thirty years—first with

Vladimir Shileiko, a former tutor for the Sheremetevs, and then later in a communal apartment; during the Soviet period, the poet worked as a street sweeper and yardkeeper.

The Petersburg Metro opened in 1955. It is one of the deepest subway systems in the world and was conceived as a kind of underground cathedral to communism.

Interlude: Second Letter (Never Sent) to G.

When I asked Gandlevsky why he memorized his poems, he told me that he did not memorize them. He wrote them in his head, line by line, over the course of many days. Sometimes it took him months to finish one.

Fourteenth. Outside Kresti Prison

Based on an elaborately carved clock representing the hut of Baba Yaga.

Baba Yaga is a witch whose hut was known to walk on chicken legs. She lures lost children to eat them, crushing their bones in the giant mortar she rides, propelling herself with the pestle, and covering her tracks with a broomstick. She has no power over the pure of heart.

Kresti ("Crosses") Prison is the infamous prison built in 1892, where Leon Trotsky and Lev Gumilev, the son of Anna Akhmatova, were once held. Akhmatova's "Requiem" begins at the gates of Kresti Prison in 1935. In 2002, the derelict building housed more than seven thousand inmates, with one thousand infected with tuberculosis and fourteen hundred with H.I.V.

Interlude: Letter to Petersburg

Piskariovsky Cemetery is a memorial to the victims of the Siege of Leningrad during World War II.

"to burn posthumously, like a word" is from a poem by Arseny Tarkovsky.

Fifteenth. Vereshchagin's *Doors*

Based on monumental gate... inspired by an ambitious design that was submitted for a competition but never built...

Vasily Vereshchagin, born into St. Petersburg aristocracy, pursued a career in the military and in painting. He fought with the imperial army in the Caucasus and painted scenes from life in Turkestan.

Coda: At the Dump with Van Gogh's *Peach Tree in Blossom*

Vincent Van Gogh, to his brother Theo: "You have been suffering to see your youth pass like a drift of smoke."

See also *The Icon and the Axe* by James Billington, *Natasha's Dance: A Cultural History of Russia* by Orlando Figes, *Sunlight at Midnight: St. Petersburg and the Rise of Modern Russia* by W. Bruce Lincoln, *The 900 Days: The Siege of Leningrad* by Harrison Salisbury, and *Petersburg: A Cultural History* by Solomon Volkov.

[Ambient Noise]
Header: Scaffolding
Tip of the cap to Andy Clark, thanks to Jessica Lewis Luck.

Footer: Hermitage (A Spectroscopy)
For Amy Breau and John Patton.

Acknowledgments

My great gratitude to Amy Breau, for her steadfastness and careful critiques. To our girls, Adele and Leila, for the joy they bring.

Thanks to Simeon Berry (*il miglior fabbro*), David Adams, Danny Caine, Michael Dumanis, Sarah Gridley, Dave Lucas, E. J. McAdams, and Paula McLain for their critiques on earlier versions of this book.

Thanks to Maxine Chernoff for seeing *Pictures* as a worthy journey in language and choosing it for the Akron Poetry Prize.

Thanks to Eduard Gordeev for the photograph on the cover; to Amy Freels for her clever design; and to Mary Biddinger, series editor and general encourager of the Akron Series in Poetry.

Grateful acknowledgment is also due to John Carroll University, the National Endowment for the Arts, the Community Partnership for Arts and Culture, and the Ohio Arts Council, for providing fellowships that gave me time to write.

Shout-outs to fellow Petersburg travelers—Kim Addonizio, Nathan Deuel, Sergey Gandlevsky, Andrea Gregovich, Mikhail Iossel, Michael Leong, Gina Ochsner, Jeff Parker, and Andrei Zorin—whose presences are felt in this work.

Grateful acknowledgment is also due to the following journals for publishing versions of these poems: *1913: A Journal of Forms, Angle, Crazyhorse, Diagram, FIELD, Jacket, New American Writing, Plume, P-Queue, Redactions, Santa Clara Review, Sierra Nevada Review, Sukoon, Truck,* and *Upstreet.*

Philip Metres is the author of a number of books, including *Sand Opera* (2015), *I Burned at the Feast: Selected Poems of Arseny Tarkovsky* (2015), *A Concordance of Leaves* (2013), *To See the Earth* (2008), and *Behind the Lines: War Resistance Poetry on the American Homefront since 1941* (2007). His work has garnered a Lannan Fellowship, two NEA fellowships, five Ohio Arts Council Grants, the George W. Hunt, S.J. Prize, the Beatrice Hawley Award, two Arab American Book Awards, the Watson Fellowship, the Creative Workforce Fellowship, the Cleveland Arts Prize and the PEN/Heim Translation Fund grant. He is professor of English at John Carroll University in Cleveland. http://www.philipmetres.com